ZOMBIE
LIFE CYCLES

by Noah Leatherland

Minneapolis, Minnesota

Credits
All images courtesy of Shutterstock.com. With thanks to Getty Images, Thinkstock Photo, and iStockphoto. Cover – tsuneomp, Sergio Photone, Here, Jakub Krechowicz, sociologas, wabeno. Recurring – Elizaveta Mironets, sociologas, wabeno. P1 – tsuneomp. P4–5 – Pavlo Baliukh, Romolo Tavani. P6–7 – Bob Krist, Leo Lintang. P8–9 – Public Domain/Wikimedia, FOTOKITA. P10–11 – DimaBerlin, motortion. P12–13 – Joelee Creative, Paulo Cesar Ayres. P14–15 – Edit 4 Me, FOTOKITA. P16–17 – Maris Grunskis, N. Steele. P18–19 – Kiselev Andrey Valerevich, Morphius Film. P20–21 – Nebojsa Markovic, Deborah Kolb. P22–23 – Tithi Luadthong, Pascal-L-Marius. P24–25 – Stepan Kapl, FOTOKITA. P26–27 – pressmaster, leolintang. P28–29 – Choksawatdikorn, Kiselev Andrey Valerevich. P30 – Fer Gregory.

Bearport Publishing Company Product Development Team
President: Jen Jenson; Director of Product Development: Spencer Brinker; Managing Editor: Allison Juda; Associate Editor: Naomi Reich; Associate Editor: Tiana Tran; Art Director: Colin O'Dea; Designer: Kim Jones; Designer: Kayla Eggert; Product Development Assistant: Owen Hamlin

Library of Congress Cataloging-in-Publication Data is available at www.loc.gov or upon request from the publisher.

ISBN: 979-8-89232-059-7 (hardcover)
ISBN: 979-8-89232-533-2 (paperback)
ISBN: 979-8-89232-192-1 (ebook)

© 2025 BookLife Publishing
This edition is published by arrangement with BookLife Publishing.

North American adaptations © 2025 Bearport Publishing Company. All rights reserved. No part of this publication may be reproduced in whole or in part, stored in any retrieval system, or transmitted in any form or by any means, electronic, mechanical, photocopying, recording, or otherwise, without written permission from the publisher. Bearport Publishing is a division of Chrysalis Education Group.

For more information, write to Bearport Publishing, 5357 Penn Avenue South, Minneapolis, MN 55419.

CONTENTS

WHAT IS A LIFE CYCLE? 4
WHAT IS A ZOMBIE? 6
BECOMING A ZOMBIE 8
THE EARLY ZOMBIE. 10
THE FULLY TRANSFORMED ZOMBIE. 12
DIET 14
ON THE MOVE 16
THE OLD ZOMBIE 18
FROM FOOD TO ZOMBIE 20
TYPES OF ZOMBIES 22
SPOTTING A ZOMBIE 24
HOW TO DEAL WITH A ZOMBIE. 26
LIFE CYCLE OF A ZOMBIE 28
BEWARE THE PARANORMAL! 30
GLOSSARY 31
INDEX 32
READ MORE 32
LEARN MORE ONLINE 32

WHAT IS A LIFE CYCLE?

Every living thing has a life cycle. Over this cycle, a living thing changes and grows. It might look different at each stage of life.

Eventually, most living things die. They **reproduce** to keep the cycle going even after they are gone. This is a normal part of living.

But what about creatures that are **paranormal**? Surely these beings would have a beginning, middle, and end to life, too. These steps may just be different than what we see in the real world.

People often explain scary or unusual things by telling stories. Sometimes, the stories have very strange creatures!

What would a zombie life cycle be like? Let's imagine. . . .

WHAT IS A ZOMBIE?

Zombies have terrified people for a long time. Stories about dead creatures coming back to life have been told for thousands of years.

These stories are not always the same. But they often describe the creatures in a similar way. Most importantly, zombies are not alive. Their hearts do not beat. Yet their bodies still move around Earth. They are often called the walking dead.

Many think legends of these beings go back to the zombis of Vodou. Vodou is a traditional Afro-Haitian religion.

A zombie's dead body is said to break apart as it moves. Often, these rotting creatures lose pieces of themselves as they go.

Somehow, a zombie's brain is said to work just enough to keep the creature shuffling around. According to most legends, zombies are driven by one thing. They want food.

BECOMING A ZOMBIE

Different legends talk of different ways zombies are made. In all of the stories, however, zombies start out as living, breathing humans. Then, they die.

Some stories say zombies are dead bodies being controlled by magic. In other tales, zombies are made after a big **disaster**. Some say the harm from an **atomic bomb** could make zombies.

Bomb explosion

Many stories say zombies are made by a **virus**.

Rabies is a deadly virus. It can be spread to humans through the bite of a sick animal.

Often, this virus is spread by other zombies. A person turns into a zombie after being bitten by one of the scary creatures. This makes some sense. Many illnesses can be spread through blood or **saliva**.

THE EARLY ZOMBIE

In some stories, a person becomes a zombie in seconds. In others, the person does not **transform** into the creature for hours or days.

If the change were caused by a virus, people would probably feel sick first. They might act as if they had a cold or the flu. They could get a fever. They may cough or get a runny nose.

The beginning?

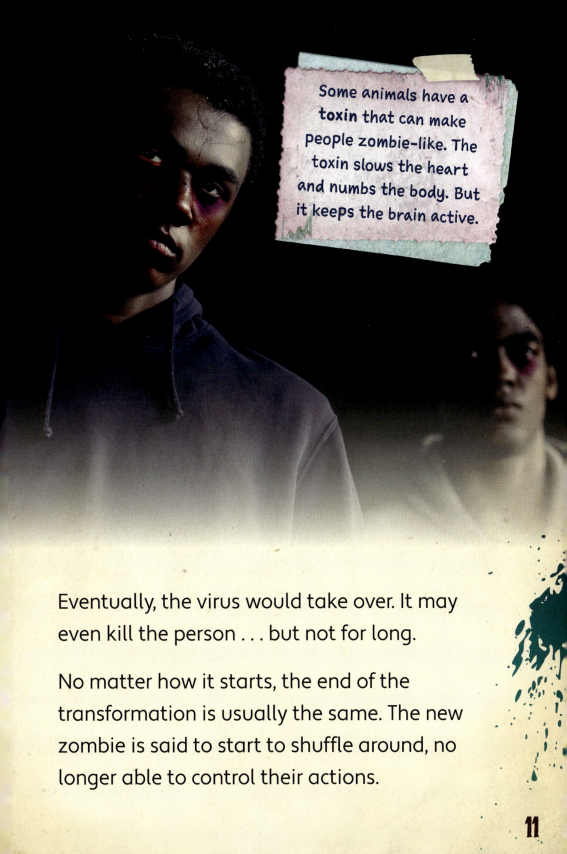

Some animals have a **toxin** that can make people zombie-like. The toxin slows the heart and numbs the body. But it keeps the brain active.

Eventually, the virus would take over. It may even kill the person . . . but not for long.

No matter how it starts, the end of the transformation is usually the same. The new zombie is said to start to shuffle around, no longer able to control their actions.

THE FULLY TRANSFORMED ZOMBIE

Zombies are said to be able to move around because their brains still work after death. However, that's where the brainpower stops. Most stories agree that zombies cannot think for themselves.

Instead, like many animals, zombies are probably led by **instinct**. Zombies are only in search of something to eat.

Zombies might look weak, but their instincts are strong. Their bodies may be, too, if they are freshly dead.

As the stories go, zombies will stop at nothing to get a bite.

The zombie-ant fungus grows inside ants. It takes control of the ants' bodies. Then, it eats them from the inside out.

Fungus

DIET

In most stories, zombies shuffle along in search of something to eat. What makes up a zombie's diet? Usually, zombies are thought to eat people!

Zombies are said to eat every part of a person they can. They will chomp through skin, muscles, and bones. In some stories, a zombie's favorite part is the brain.

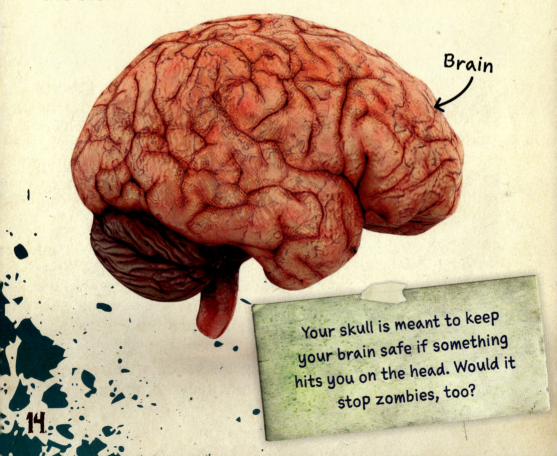

Brain

Your skull is meant to keep your brain safe if something hits you on the head. Would it stop zombies, too?

When living things eat food, their bodies **digest** it.

A zombie's stomach and intestines would not work because its body is dead. So, the zombie's meal would just sit inside its stomach, slowly rotting away.

ON THE MOVE

Since zombies are not alive, they could probably survive almost anywhere. Extreme weather would not stop them. They could live in the hottest heat or coolest cold.

Dawn of the Dead was a popular zombie movie from 1978. A lot of it took place in a shopping mall.

Some stories say zombies visit the places they went when they were alive. If a person liked to go shopping, they might hang around shopping malls as a zombie.

Wherever they went, zombies probably wouldn't stay in one place for long. The creatures move around in search of food. So, zombies would probably be where lots of humans could be found.

If zombies were all looking for the same thing, they would probably meet up with others. Would a large group of zombies have a name similar to a group of animals? Perhaps they would be called a herd.

A herd of zombies?

THE OLD ZOMBIE

Unlike many creatures, zombies would not grow bigger or stronger as they got older. In fact, they would break down because their bodies are already dead.

Zombies would probably start to rot. **Bacteria** eats away at living things once they die. This would make zombies look like a gory mess.

Bacteria can't stop this zombie!

A person's skeleton is held together by the muscles and skin around it. So, as a zombie's body rots, their skeleton would come apart, too. Eventually, a zombie's arms and legs may fall off.

After a few years, a zombie would barely have any body left. However, the stories say zombies keep going as long as they have brains.

Over time, dead animals break down into dirt. This feeds plants.

FROM FOOD
TO ZOMBIE

Some stories say zombies can go on looking for food forever. When they catch sight of something they can bite a chunk out of, they do not stop.

Zombies would be especially dangerous in a group. Many zombies coming together could surround buildings and break through barriers.

The real danger when coming face to face with a zombie would not be becoming a meal. If the stories are true, it would be becoming a zombie yourself.

According to legends, a zombie's bite does not need to be very deep. As long as their rotten teeth break through the skin, their would-be meal could become a zombie.

Animals that eat only meat usually have long, sharp teeth. This makes it easier for them bite into other animals.

TYPES OF ZOMBIES

What would make a zombie even more dangerous?

FAST ZOMBIES

A fast zombie would be especially scary. Imagine if someone who was quick when they were alive became part of the walking dead.

Or maybe if a zombie grew very hungry it would run. The zombie's speed would mean it could catch more to eat.

The fastest person on Earth can sprint at speeds more than 27 miles per hour (44 kph).

SMART ZOMBIES

What if a person who was very smart were turned into a zombie? Would they be smarter than most mindless zombies?

Even remembering how to do basic things could make a zombie dangerous. They could think of ways to get at their next meal.

SPOTTING A ZOMBIE

Although it might be easy to spot a zombie that is falling apart, a freshly bitten zombie may be hard to notice. What could you look for?

EYES

Some stories say a zombie's eyes are blank and cloudy. This may be because their body is dying.

SMELL

Use your nose! If someone smells rotten, they might be a zombie.

Dead bodies let off a smelly gas as they break down.

MOUTH

If someone's mouth is hanging open, they might be getting ready to bite. Remember, according to the stories, this is all zombies think about.

GROANS

A zombie's brain is only useful for finding food. This means zombies wouldn't be able to speak. All they may be able to do is grunt and groan.

HOW TO DEAL WITH A ZOMBIE

The walking dead would be hard to get rid of. After all, they are already dead.

Things that might hurt other creatures probably would not harm a zombie. Zombies are said to not feel any pain.

You could not poison, stab, or even set a zombie on fire to kill it.

Stories say the only way to stop a zombie is to get rid of its brain. If you want to make sure the zombie is done for, take off its head. Without it, there would be no brain-body connection.

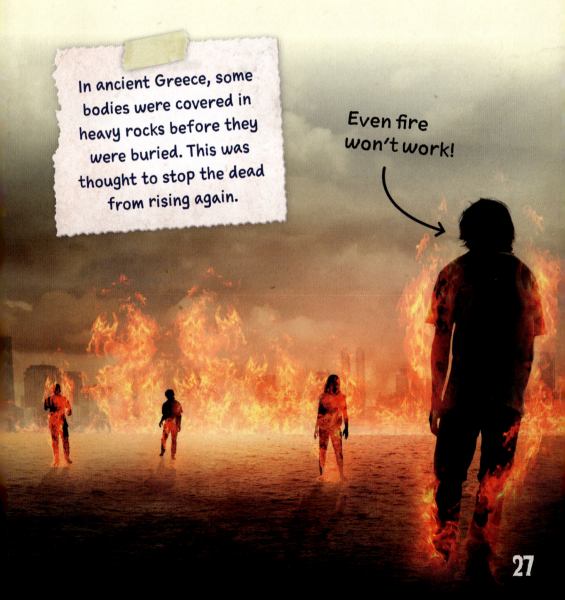

In ancient Greece, some bodies were covered in heavy rocks before they were buried. This was thought to stop the dead from rising again.

Even fire won't work!

LIFE CYCLE OF A ZOMBIE

So, what would the life cycle of a zombie look like? The bite from a zombie may start the transformation from human to walking dead. At first, the person might just feel sick.

Soon enough, they will die . . . though, according the stories, they are not quite dead. Then, the hunger begins. All the zombie would think about is eating humans.

A tiny creature called a wheel animal can freeze and come back to life later. Scientists have brought back one wheel animal from 24,000 years ago!

Peeling skin

A zombie's body might start to rot even as it walks around. Its skin could peel off and its guts might fall out in a bloody mess. It might lose an arm, a leg, or both!

As it rots away, a zombie might bite an unlucky person. This is said to continue the cycle.

BEWARE THE PARANORMAL!

There are stories around the world of all sorts of paranormal creatures. If you want to learn more, be very careful. . . .

Zombies may be scary, but what if there is something even worse creeping around in the dark? How would its paranormal life cycle begin, continue, and end?

GLOSSARY

atomic bomb a very powerful bomb that can destroy entire cities

bacteria tiny living things that can sometimes cause disease

digest to break down food inside the body

disaster something that happens suddenly and causes much damage or loss

instinct things an animal does or knows naturally, without having to learn

legends stories that are handed down from the past

paranormal things that are not able to be explained by science

reproduce to make more of a living thing

saliva the liquid in the mouths of humans and other animals

toxin a poison that can cause harm to plants and animals

transform to change into something else

virus a tiny thing that causes diseases in people and other animals

INDEX

bacteria 18
bite 9, 13, 20–21, 24–25, 28–29
brains 7, 11–12, 14, 19, 25, 27
death 4, 6–9, 12–13, 15–16, 18–19, 22, 24, 26–28
food 7, 15, 17, 20, 25
groans 25
herds 17
instinct 12–13
mouth 25
rot 7, 15, 18–19, 21, 24, 29
saliva 9
skin 14, 19, 21, 29
smell 24
teeth 21

READ MORE

Erickson, Marty. *Zombies (Legendary Creatures).* Mankato, MN: The Child's World, 2022.

Redshaw, Hermione. *The Night of the Zombies (Supernatural Survivor).* Minneapolis: Bearport Publishing Company, 2023.

LEARN MORE ONLINE

1. Go to **www.factsurfer.com** or scan the QR code below.

2. Enter **"Zombie Life Cycle"** into the search box.

3. Click on the cover of this book to see a list of websites.